Mike Kelley

Hello God It's Me Again
By
Mike Kelley

Mike Kelley

HELLO GOD, IT' ME AGAIN
MIKE KELLEY

Published By Parables
September, 2019

All Rights Reserved. No part of this book may be reproduced or utilized in any form or by any means, electronic or mechanical, including photocopying, recording, or by any information storage and retrieval system, without permission in writing from the author.

ISBN **978-1-951497-02-6**
Printed in the United States of America

Readers should be aware that Internet Web sites offered as citations and/or sources for further information may have been changed or disappeared between the time this was written and the time it is read.

Hello God It's Me Again

By

Mike Kelley

Mike Kelley

Hello God, it's me again

Just looking back over my life
Sometimes I do this when the years change numbers
Been thinking about where I wasn't
It seems to be a lot when you hook it together
Wasn't there when my Grand-Pa passed
Then again when Grand-Ma too
Even my own Mom and Dad left this earth without my goodbye
My Brother's wife, my Sister's Husband and her son too
Then another Brothers son
It's a powerful weight to carry just holding these losses
I've been on a lot of trails, always gone without purpose
Some driven, some walked, even some, just crawled along
Slipped in mud, snow, Ice and fell over rocks
Winds blew, Rains washed, even went to war
I walked with the dust of years on my boots
Been shot, cut, beat on, burned, and broken
Spit out blood, and cried warm tears, Darn near drown and fell from some high places
Scars from ever silly thing and you know them all

Sometimes I wonder why you keep me on this side of the sun
I suppose there's a purpose yet, I'm too blind to see
Got this here New Year coming
New calendars with new numbers
We mostly mark off the years since your boy was taken
Yet, he's not gone
Lord, I must sound like a tired old man just rambling
I've been gone all my life it seems but never alone
Never knew that everywhere I went he was there
I suppose he wore out a few boots just tagging along
So where ever I will be gone in this next year
I'll try a bit harder to follow him
And just maybe I won't be too gone
That's it, Lord,
A-Men

Hello God, It's Me Agaain

Hello God, it's me again

Just got the word about another soul lifted up
Seems sad and happy
Sad to let go from the earth
Happy that the folks in Heaven got another good man
I wish for the family here on this earth to know peace
To find comfort that a loved one no longer suffers
You know it is like they are on a trip in some ways
Just gone down the road
We are all on that same road
And we will be reunited in times ahead
Till we do we will recall them with love
Our thoughts like postcards will come
You give us life Lord and we are blessed to share it with others
That is a treasure and a blessing
Give us our tears of loss, but dry them with the memories
Surprise us with something from their life
Something that will make us smile till we see them again
Hold dear to the earthly family
You know our hearts will last longer than the flowers that wilt

Send down a warm knowing
One that tells us the soul has arrived at your door
That your blessing will now be unfolded unto that one so loved
Thanks God, for the way this all works out
It makes things seem like a reunion ahead
Just beyond the river when we are all on the other side.
Yes, we shall gather at the river
That's my prayer
A-men

Hello God, it's me again

Well here we are on Veteran's Day
Now I feel a warm tear in this memory
Folks around offer me a free cup of coffee
A sandwich at no cost
They say thank you for my service
But, something dark inside me cries
I am no hero for what was done
Dark are the memories within
Tears come for those that didn't come home
Tears also for those that were taken by our actions
For me it was Vietnam
Such a lovely country
People that I never knew
Yet folks you gave life to
For others in this world too
Places and people outside our country
From our land brothers and sisters have put on the uniforms
Taking up a mission to defend our homeland
America we cry
Home of the free, the brave, the mighty
But, Lord we are just people

Made in your image
Why must we fight?
Can we not find a better way?
We call ourselves "One Nation Under God"
And, "In God We Trust"
Yet today those words are fading
Our own government strikes them from the documents
Words from our Founding Fathers
You know I am a simple soul
I don't understand this all
Yet I salute those that stand to protect our way of life
A way of freedom to bend our knees and pray
A freedom to serve for God and Country
And I pray that the country remembers you in our missions
I am an old man and fight no more
My day of such is over and I must account for my doings
I will not take up a free coffee
Nor will I take the sandwich
The thank you for a service is to be written in the book of life
The one with which you are the judge
Well, God, I may have said too much of this
But hold them all
The folks that defend and may they never need to fire a shot
Bring them home in peace
And, forgive us that did find a shot fired
A-Men

Hello God, it's me again

Seems life is always in change
Each season falls as you lay plans
The seeding of the cat-tails lift to the winds
I watched them float in the breezes
Each little speck of life you watch over
Some will take root and be the offspring of the mother
The wonders of your creation only you know

Tonight, I lift a prayer for a seed of a lifetime ago
Back in the days when I ran lost in this world
Back to a time when two lives met under your hand
One going east, one west both destined to collide
A path across a lonely Texas road
It was maybe not a chance meeting at all
As the winds and darkness came in nature
Both we found the darkness and winds in our minds
Unsettled skies bring rain in nature
Unsettled hearts bring tears in lifetime

I need not tell you the story Lord

You know it may be better than my recall
Like a seed in the wind from the cat-tails
You know when it is cast
So, the same in life

I send up a prayer this night into the midnight sky
Beyond the moon, and stars
Beyond this world
To your door
My prayer for a purpose in that blowing seed
One that took root and grew
Bless us everyone with the understanding

A-Men

Hello God, it's me again

This now is the time of Thanksgiving
I am thankful for so much in this life
And am blessed in so many ways
You know my life, and all my faults and sins
I need not hide that
Yet, I still cry some over them
Now I worry that I have caused others to fall
Things I should have done, that didn't get done
Things I let happen, that should not
Today I lift this prayer for others
Some, blood of my blood
Some, I have connected with otherwise
I cannot erase my past, nor would you have me
It is what has brought me to this place I am
With all the wrong turns and detours
Use my example of how not to do things
Let the folks I have wronged in this life
See me clearly with my shortcomings
I stand at your door at times, knocking
Then you open the door with love
Show them all that love

This Thanksgiving I pray with tears
Thankful and heartbroken too
Thankful that you have given me direction
And Heartbroken for those without
Those in my thoughts you know
Well I know I am lower than the dust on my boots
But if you can help along those that are stumbling
Help them to the path of living life
Then that is what I wish to give thanks for
This is my lefthanded thanksgiving prayer
A-Men

Hello God, it's me again

Taps

Memorial Day

To the Red, White, and Blue
To the Stars of the States
Not for one State but them all
United for the Country
The South, North, East, and West
To the brave that did the most
To those who bled for freedom
Those men and women
Those uniforms of honor
Those coffins covered with the Colors of the Nation
The Fallen
Stand us at their markers
Let our shadows fall over their soil
Let our voices lift in prayer
Let our hearts be touched by their efforts
We lay a flower and tear

Let us recall
Names on walls of service given
Where do they come from?
Our homes
Our neighbors
Our country
They take nothing from this world
But they gave so much for the living
Let us recall
Let us remember their faces
Let not them be lost to our memory
Taps have been played
Bodies have been laid
All in the name of Freedom
Hold them in your hands
Give them the peace they left for our world
May their souls remain in your kingdom
And to you dear God
Bless America
This is my Prayer
A-Men

Hello God, it's me again

Please excuse the tears and a shaky voice
My heart is praying for others
Seems folks are losing their way in this world
Some close to my heart
Rain is falling across the fields today
Some falling inside the houses that were once homes
Hearts being separated by indifferences
You know there was love there once
It sparkled and shined
But the past came whipping back
Like a horse bucking
It takes some kind of Cowboy to hold on then
Some just let go, I did that a time or two
I have a saddle bag filled with bad decisions
But I also have a beat-up bible in there too
Those words tell what to do with a history
And it tells me also about the future
Lord I live in the now of my life
Not looking to impress the world
Yet I see on the trail some I love caught up in life

Looking for answers I can't give
Hold them a bit closer if you can
Untangle the ropes in their minds
Open their eyes to what they must do
If their hearts are so broken
And their spirit so bruised give them a new pasture
Let them move on as they may need
But if there is a ray of hope
One ounce of love that remains remind them of that
Dust them off, and shake them up
Then send them home
That's my prayer
A-men

Hello God, it's me again

Just about as hot as I might get
But thankful none the less
I cheated the Devil again
He and his fires of hell
Someday he might just get me
Yet I just don't like the smoke and fire
Oh, I suppose there are other ways
But I don't open those doors
Kicking off my boots now
Shaking away the dust
Sweat been dripping all too long
Need a splash in the creek
You know them waters got those snakes
So that's my prayer
Could you hold them off for a bit?
Just long enough for a cool bath
Tomorrow trail to be even hotter I'm told
Would like to start off fresh
Well that's its Lord I hate to be a bother
If it's too much trouble I take with me a knife
A-Men

Mike Kelley

Hello God, It's Me Agaain

Hello God, it's me again

I know we have been talking a lot lately
It is like riding a bull in a rodeo
You can get on one ok
But it is the kick and fall that hurts
My old boots are still dusty from the last round
As bad as it can be there is always the next
To try to hold on till the bell rings
Life is like that bull ride at times
We grab the rope and hold on
But before the bell rings our heart is broken
The fall is one thing
But getting stepped on, well that really hurts
Yet somehow, we get up a bit winded
Spit out a little blood and dirt
Then find a clean shirt and dust off the hat
Climb back on
Just wishing to hear the sound of the bell
That bell that tells you, you made it
Tonight, I am praying for another
One that needs to hear the bell too
One that has been stepped on

Face down in the dirt
And needs to shake it off
Just take a hand before the bull comes back
lift this one to safety
Let it be the bells in life to ring
Thanks God,
A-Men

Hello God, it's me again

Just looking out to the day ahead
Coffee brewing if you want a cup
Thought if you got a minute to talk a bit
You know they say not to mix politics and religion
I suppose that is why so many politicians are the way they
are
No, I am not judging them that's a job for you
I am just saying it is hard to understand at vote time
Folks say they will do right then they don't
They say they are working for us
But they don't
Seems a game to them like playing cards
They get the money and we don't even get a deal
It worries me Lord everything seems to be about money
The small farmers are about gone
Heck, the home of my parents too, it's all blacktopped over
with airplanes where we used to pick blackberries
I don't understand this land thing, you made this earth, gave
it to us to live on and all over the world people are fighting

over it. It goes back to the early days even before the bible was written up.

I think the Native Americans had it right they didn't own land they lived on it and respected it, the same as water and air, but it was the folks that came to this country for freedom that took it away from them and moved them to places beyond so they could have it. Then again and again they were moved. Kingdoms fought for the dirt of the earth so they could be bigger, more powerful, but for what end?

God, I am not asking nothing for me, just for wisdom to find that politician that understands we are just visitors here, this is your world and it has nothing to do with land, being bigger, more powerful, or money. You gave us Mosses to deliver a nation and he did, then you gave us Jesus to deliver the world.

I guess it would be too much to ask for someone to let us deliver ourselves in sharing what we already have till comes the time when the meek take over the earth, but if there is someone to look towards point us in the right direction.

Well the coffee is all gone time to kick out and find my way past all the political signs and make something of this day.

Thanks, God, for listening

A-Men

Hello God, It's Me Agaain

Hello God, it's me again

I had a dream last night
I was no longer me
I was the last leaf of winter
Just holding on in the cold
Then I heard the branch when it spoke
Let go it said, your time is over
Even the words made me shiver
Then winds blew with a frozen breath
Yet I held tight
Then came the storm of the season
Snow and Ice
I heard the branch cry and crack
It was I that told the branch to hold on
As it twisted in pain
Hold on, old branch, hold on
That day passed with frozen rain
Then snow
Then came more
I told the branch the season comes with numbers
Days man call it
We counted together through the day

Then the night
Then it was that every branch lifted to the heavens
Sending out a prayer
Each one the same
Each one asking for strength
Then came the night when clouds parted
Silver showers of moonlight
It came to the branches
It came to me
We counted away the pain
We found spring together
And new life came to the cold earth
New leaves started to unfold
I held on all winter
As did the branch
Then I was released to the warm breezes
Floating on waves of air
With a last breath I lay upon the new grass
It was there that he came
A boy of school
He picked me up and spoke
He told me to hold on
As he carried me away
He placed me in a page of wax
And then I became his work of class
He was to grow and become a man of nature
And I was the one he chose as the first
I am still holding on

Hello God, It's Me Agaain

Now under glass in a library
A window close allows me a view
Outside to the world
Outside stands the tree
And a branch that has grown strong

I know you send down dreams
So many have filtered in my sleep
Some quickly left in dawns light
Others hold tight like the leaf
The meanings unfold to my mind
As you have planted its seed

Thanks, for the dream
A-Men

Mike Kelley

Hello God, it's me again

Winter's breath is cold right now
Old home creaks with every new day
Old Bones too
It is a tough one it seems
Yet the good book tells me I can handle it
This January has brought me to my knees
We are about to move into the Valentine month
I pray that it is warm with love and hope
I cried last night in the dark
Feeling a bit lost I guess
But then Jesus cried once too
Don't have time to write much it seems
I guess just this prayer lifted is the best I can do
It's a long road ahead yet
I got to ride it without human help in my job
Yet, I know you are with me like a shadow
So I will saddle up and chinch it tight
Then ride on down the fence row again
It is you and me, Lord
I just pray to be a good sidekick to you

Well that's my Getty up go
Just wanted to let my friends know all is well
Just won't much be seen of or heard from for another month
Keep them all safe God
Hold them with all in your hands
All my brothers and sisters, sons and daughters
All those who might think I am dead or in jail
Just let them know I'll see them all in my dreams
Thanks, Lord
A-Men

Hello God, it's me again

It's Sunday and here I am
Just you, Rope, and me
Not many folks understand a dog in church
Out here under the clouds is our church
But Rope, well he is special
Seems he is a Guardian Angel
Can't count the times he flushed out rattlers
Keeping me and the horse on a clear path
Were out here all alone, sept for you
But it's Sunday and here we are in your hands
Got my bible to read Rope the story of Noah
He looked like he might know that one
Maybe some of his family from them days
Sure, is a blessing to have my dog Rope
Next to you he's the best friend I got
I trust him with my life
Today we will break bread together
I'll share with him the story of Jesus and the Lords Supper
Don't suppose there was beans and cornbread back then

Yet it will be just as blessed over our grace spoken
Later maybe my harmonica might find a tune
Some notes for Amazing Grace
Rope likes that one
Won't be many others here in church today I guess
There is an eagle up yonder
Maybe a jackrabbit or two in the brush
So, here's my prayer up to your house
It's a prayer of thanks
Thanks for this day and holding me upright in the saddle
For the cool breeze that sings over the prairie grasses
For sun that sits in that blue sky
For my friend Rope keep him as he keeps me
Well that's its Lord time to kick up the campfire coffee
Your welcome to a cup if you like it black
Got no cows-cream
Had a few lumps of brown sugar but Rope got it gone
Will set a spell now
Sending our thoughts your way
A-Men

It was there that the sun moved behind clouds as just a faint shadow of the cross remained. It was there he was to die as winds moved and a chill filled that upper hill. Winds carried the evil event as the sky darken and the ground shook. He was held in place by steel that tore at the bone and his blood came forth. Then his shadow was no more. It was lifted from the earth in his last words beyond.

Today I look to the shadow of the cross and feel it touch my soul within. It can only be seen if you believe in him as he is. No longer an image, but always the shadow remains within my heart.

Now, these many years later I feel the cold shadow of that cross that on this spring day we celebrate his return. Springtime the time when life renews is fitting as our lives are renewed by the death of the body and the return of his spirit.

Hello God, it's me again

I am awake before in the shadows of the night leaves and the day arrives
It is here I feel close as my mind finds that shadow of the cross
The bells of Sunday will ring today
A call to remembrance
Your houses will fill with those that worship maybe just this one day
This day I lift my prayer not with a shine on my boots
No tie or white shirt do I even own
This is what others see as the costume of worship
Heck Lord you know me the man with holes in his pockets
I don't fit in refinery
I do however wrap myself with respect and worship as I am
This Easter I find myself praying a prayer of thanks for all that was given in the shadow of the cross

I was not there when he was nailed
Nor when they placed him in the tomb
But I am here today sending up my words that this old world
could not hold the Savior of mankind
I am here giving thanks for the shadow.
A-Men

Mike Kelley

Hello God, it's me again

This is a prayer of thanks
In the Valley of The Shadow
He that walked in the valley
With that shadow of death so close
Hath been to a golden door
Yet, returned

Prayers were lifted
For his will to be done
Voices cried with love
As, that Greater Spirit listened

He the giver of life
Return that soul to live
Restoring his feet upon this earth
To open his eyes from a greater horizon

It is so great a treasure
Life itself lifted up
A man has a purpose
Yet ahead to unfold

And she who loves him
Sees within, a gift from God
Two hands united
In paths of life restored

To be at that moment
Where just beyond, a step away
The book of life is opened
A soul is restored, in salvation

We, who have bent our knees
Lifted our prayers with tears
Rejoice in this new sunrise
For we have felt the hand of God

In that valley of the shadow
darkness fades away
As written in the Psalms
Thou art with us all

Again, we bend our knees
lifting our voices in thanksgiving
For miracles and mercies given
And, he our brother returned

Thanks God
A-Men

Hello God, it's me again

It is a sad darkens that falls
This old world finds yet more to pray about
Tears rain down from faces, looking for answers
To the night we light our candles
Lifting thoughts with words to a Greater Spirit
Hands shake, in the shadow of fear
Fear not for themselves, but others
Those that are fallen, without reason
Across our globe they fall
A world out of control
Tomorrows sun will lift again
Yet, mankind will remember
Arms will fold around loved ones
Holding to the love within
We are here for a purpose, everyone
This earth is not our destiny
It will be found beyond
Beyond the sunrises, and sunsets
Beyond the tears
Beyond the sadness of today
When we are called, we leave the dust behind

Mike Kelley

Our boots lay empty
Yet our feet will walk a higher ground
I will not allow this sadness, to take control
My candle burns its light even in the wind
My heart is given in faith
There within is hope, love, and answers
This world cannot take that away
No matter how evil, may be found in this life
There is goodness yet to find
Goodness to share
Thanks for the goodness
A-Men

Hello God, it's me again

Cold winter winds blow today
Across frozen grounds they whisper
Lonely, comes the voice of winter
Skies hold to a gray and silver cast
It is here the voice inside comes as a thought
Some forgotten days that have past, come again
Faces of those you know again you see
Their words lift to your ear, memories return
The oak stand naked after falls harvest
Yet, you see the leaves of summer, and a picnic awaiting
Voices happy, as you take that hand you love so well
A kiss exchanged
Children fly kites running through tall grasses
Then again blows that cruel wind
They are gone your hand is empty
A tear warm runs across wrinkles left in time
You look at the cold stone
The name etched with dates
Here you kneel lifting a prayer
Words you seemed to fail to say, now come
Your heart releases love

You press yourself towards the stone
You listen for the voice from beyond
As eyes, tightly closed search to see
To view again the face, the smile
Winds toss across this potter's field
As you open your eyes, and see the white of snow
Fresh and pure it comes, lightly laying to earth
You look up to the heavens
There you see a single ray of light, only for an instant
The words you spoke were received
A blessing returned
The Oak holds a coat of white across its limbs
No, the picnic is not there
But a kiss is felt upon your cheek
As love never dies
Thanks, God, for the memory
A-Men

Hello God, it's me again

December holds cold a hand out as its last few hours will soon be a history of another years passing. Mist of wet spray fills the air with icy winds blowing. This now in its dying hour fades with the numbers on a calendar as sands falling in an hourglass mark time. January is ready to reach out and start another season in a new winter, one with a warm home fire burning as its smoke rises to horizons and mixes with specks of snow dancing with dreams. From my window there is no moon light on this night no welcome star do I see. Darkness looms with this exchange from old and new, here history and future dance but a second then kiss in parting. From dusk of December to dawn January we will change when that midnight second arrives. Lips may kiss, arms may embrace, and tears may fall in memory of events passing, yet hearts will search with love for what may be in this birth tonight. Tomorrows awaking will have change to it, a change within our minds as new dreams and plans are cast with prayer of hope. We are time travelers again stepping out into paths with new numbers written in time to those pages of our lives. With now my sad tired eyes I close them in dreams and pray to awake in the glow of tomorrows new year.

Good night Lord,

A-Men

Hello God, it's me again

Just looking out into the night
The slightest noise can be trouble you know
Dogs good at hearing
Once happened up on a wildcat
But Dog saved me from harm on that one
I'm not as brave as Daniel was in the lion's den
That's why I am talking with you
I get spooked sometimes
I believe you will watch over me ok
But just want to remind you where we are
There's bears out here in this area
They can do some powerful harm
It is time for me to turn in soon
And if you got an angel to look around the mountain
I'd be most pleased
And if I fall asleep and a bear comes and eats me
Can you open one of them gates in heaven and let me run in
Well that's its Lord
See you tomorrow one way or another
Good night God
A-Men

Mike Kelley

Hello God, it's me again,

Rain falling a bit hard tonight
I am not complaining none
This old dry soil needs a drink
It was so warm before that I find it a bit refreshing
For that I thank you
I got out a plate of beans here
Just can't seem to find a want to eat
I sit listening to the water splash around
Dancing off the rocks and my saddle
Kind of music in some ways
My old horse he doesn't seem none worse for the ware
That rain-washing trail dust off must feel good
We will be moving on soon
No campfire tonight
I'll miss looking up to Mr. Moon tonight
And no star will get a wish but there always tomorrow
I recall when it rains the story of Noah and his boat
Now that was a rain
Won't be needing a boat here
Just ride up to the high country

I'll set up camp down around Pine mountain I'll sleep then
Got that tarp and it will work out well
Be talking to you then in my night prayers
Till then help us if you can
Not asking you to stop the rain for us
But a bit lighter would be OK
Best be going now
Thanks for all you do Lord
And thanks for the dry socks in the saddle bag
Old boot got a hole in it
I'll get that shoe-man to fix it up in Dodge
Well beans I leave for some critter now
Find a hungry one and send it this way
Moving on,

A-Men

Hello God, it's me again

Sending Words and Wishes
It is in this life that at times, we move in a direction of change
It may be by reason of tears
And it may be to find one's self
And a means of greater peace
To this, a hand of compassion is lifted
Understanding of feelings
Wishing to bring comfort
I lift my pen to those words
Sending it to the troubled mind in conflict
Just a light from my candle I give
Let the darkness part
Find you are not alone
No, we are never alone
Sending this message to someone
A secret friend
Let not my words be lost in the winds of time
For always as long as we have a breath
A heart that beats within
We have something given to save

Hold on to the real treasures in life
Hold on to yourself
Hold on to God
A-Men

Hello God it's me again

Found this steer lost out in the wilds
There's no herd around I can see
We are miles from anywhere
I'll pack him along as best I can
Maybe a herd I'll find
It'll slow my travels a bit but I just can't cut him loose
I hope you can help me here Lord
Wait
I hear a rider coming this way
It's a trail hand looking for this guy
Sure, was a quick answer to my prayer Lord
This reminds me of the 90 and 9 and one lost
Now it's found
Your old Bible has a lot of stories in it
I keep running into new chapters everyday
Tonight, I want to read around the campfire
That old story of the shepherd
Got a can of peaches in the saddle bag
It will be a treat come days end
See you around campsite tonight
A-Men

Mike Kelley

Hello God, it's me again

One may never know the taste of dirt
But I do
I have found it face to face
Sometimes with a drop or two of blood
Sometimes slick and muddy
Sometimes dried on old boots
It's told God made man from the dirt
Darn if I don't believe it true
For when my face in down into it
That is when I am the closest to that Greater Spirit
Thanks, God, for the dirt
A-Men

Mike Kelley

Hello God, it's me again

The world has outgrown me
Seems I don't fit anymore
Old school thinking has no place today
People don't shake your hand and look into your eyes
Real friends are hard to find
People you could just talk with on the front porch
Special times were when family away came home
The State Fair had a rodeo
The drugstore had an ice cream counter
A kiss could change your life
Downtown was an adventure
Sears was a book of wishes
Furniture lasted a lifetime
Every home had a photo album with a story in every picture
Grand Parents weren't put into old folks' housings
Books were a treasure with each page turned
The family bible was always at hand
Saturday night was bath night
Sunday was church day
A mailbox sat on a post with handwritten letters

You knew all your neighbors by name and their families
If someone was in need you helped as best you could
Swear words would get your mouth washed out with Ivory soap
Now it seems swear words are in too many songs
Kids don't shoot marbles anymore or play jacks
Country roads aren't dirt anymore
Clothes and shoes were for a year
Christmas was not X-mas
Easter was a time to recall its meaning
Holidays were times with family to share
Air conditioning was an open window with a screen
The sounds of whip-poor-wills brought a smile
A treasure was finding an arrowhead and wondering its history
The American flag was in every classroom and a pledge to it spoken
The President was a man everyone trusted and could believe
Farmers were people with names, not corporations
A service station was just that, and a face of a person you knew
Homemade things were always special, made with love
Postcards were treasures in the mail with a story to tell
Life and Look were magazines that become well worn by all
There were clotheslines that gave that special outside smell to clean

Ice cold watermelons on a hot summer day under a shade tree
Any open field could become a softball game at anytime
Horseshoe pitching would make someone shout "Ringer"
Then a prayer called for everyone to say A-men and mean it
Clouds of white changing shape were wonderlands ofreams
Blackberry cobbler hot with ice cream cold still makes me smile
The sparkle of the morning due on a spider's web was a work of art
Cold mornings with hot cocoa and oatmeal around the breakfast table
There was a time a pocket knife wasn't a weapon it was a tool
Watches and clocks had to be hand wound
Ink pens didn't have ballpoints
Pencil sharpeners were hand cranks
School tablets were "Big Chief" with a picture of a Native American on the cover
We were one nation under God, and in God we trust
Valentines were given with thought and love to someone special and most handmade
The radio had tubes that would light up and bring us moments of entertainment with programs like, "The Shadow" or "Lights Out" or on the lighter side "Little Orphan Anne"
Music from the Grand O Opera, WSM out of Nashville, Tennessee

Hello God, It's Me Agaain

I still sing 16 Tons, as Tennessee Ernie Ford did
Skeeter Davis from Dry Ridge, Kentucky became a music star and Kitty Wells had a real country voice.
Baseball games you could afford to go to without taking out a loan and the hot dogs were the best
Shoot-outs were the bad guys and good guys, Roy Rogers, The Lone Ranger, and the Cisco Kid, all would win out over evil on Saturday mornings
For the world beyond was, Flash Gordon, The Green Lantern, and Superman
Things just aren't that way anymore
What was make believe is gone
No more Peter Pan and Captain Hook
No more Tom Sawyer and Huck Finn
History has put them to rest
No, I just live in a world that has outgrown me
I won't have a tale to tell any kid as they are too dull
What was is gone
I wonder if God ever looks down on us and remembers life as it used to be
Back in the days of Adam and Eve
Back when Noah was on the waters
Moses heading for that promised land
Back when this world took away his son
He must feel as I do now
The world is outgrown him
Yet we hold on,
There is always hope for a new tomorrow

Maybe an old dog, a horse, and a little land to ride
And I see the sunset with a campfire and prayer
Then as a new day comes it will be coffee with the Lord
Just thinking out loud Lord
A-Men

Hello God, it's me again

Just expressing myself
Tumbleweed in a Gypsy Wind
Looking back, it seems easy to account for the sum of one's life
The trails and paths traveled
The roads and potholes
Miles and Mountains
If where I to sum up my life
I would call myself a Tumbleweed
The winds moved me about without direction
Blowing in what I call Gypsy winds
Sure, I have regrets, don't we all?
I find now that I missed things along the way
How many boots were worn out?
There was never a pot of gold at rainbows end
I never cared much for the good life
Big house, suits, and ties
It was the dirt of the earth I found myself in
The adventure of that next hill and beyond
Had to experience the world

There were so many things to see
Seems my share of life was in the viewing and less doing
Don't get me wrong about it, that was happiness in me
So many bright sunrises and peaceful sunsets
The smell of wildflowers hidden from the world
Winds lifted me to the seas and beyond
Reflections across the waters and salt air
I shook the hand of King Neptune at the equators crossing
People greeted me in their home lands with welcome
This is my riches, treasure you keep inside
The words came to me with each treasure found
Most times captured in journals and scraps of papers
I wish to keep the secrets inside however
Those moments of something hard to understand
Moments of loss
Moments of wishing I rode the horse a bit further
The saddle held me in place as my boots weathered
No polish on them just leather scraped over rocks
Sometimes it is music in the winds
Flowing across the open spaces that bring a smile
Clouds dance in such a display
When comes the moonlight and night calls in the darkness
There is another treasure looking up to the skies
There is peace in that
It is my Holy time
A time of prayer to a Greater Spirit
He knows me and we talk freely at times
I don't talk to him like some do

Not that their words are wrong
I call upon him as I am
Just a tumbleweed in the Gypsy winds
And at the end there is a thanks for another day
I suppose I have a purpose
Just praying for wisdom
Hope someday to find it
A-Men

Mike Kelley

www.ingramcontent.com/pod-product-compliance
Lightning Source LLC
Chambersburg PA
CBHW052042280426

43661CB00085B/101